GW00502029

Virginia Woolf's childhood summer holidays spent at Talland House in St Ives not only gifted her vivid memories of the unique spirit of Cornwall – its ancient lands, wild coastal paths and mesmerising light – but also inspired her to write her masterpiece novel *To the Lighthouse*.

Using excerpts from Woolf's diaries, letters and novels, interwoven with my own artworks, this pamphlet celebrates her time in St Ives and the impact it had on her life, both as a child and as a returning adult, drawn back by poignant family memories but also perhaps the mysterious power Cornwall has over those who fall under its spell.

Writer Astra Bloom's evocative contribution finds Virginia Woolf aboard a Cornwall bound train heading from Paddington station, on Christmas Eve 1909, 'to the sea and blue gold green.'

Maggie Humm, who led the campaign for a Talland House plaque commemorating Woolf's life there, has written an insightful contribution to this pamphlet. St Ives has long been celebrated for its connection with painters and sculptors, in particular pioneering 20th century modern artists. A Virginia Woolf plaque in St Ives celebrates not just her legacy, but makes visible the inspiration of Cornwall to significant writers as well.

Louisa Amelia Albani, 2022. Artist, editor & small press publisher

Artwork: Louisa Amelia Albani, 2022.

St Ives

ZENNOR
PONIOU

TALLAND
HOUSE

GURNARD'S
HEAD

MÊN · AN · TOL

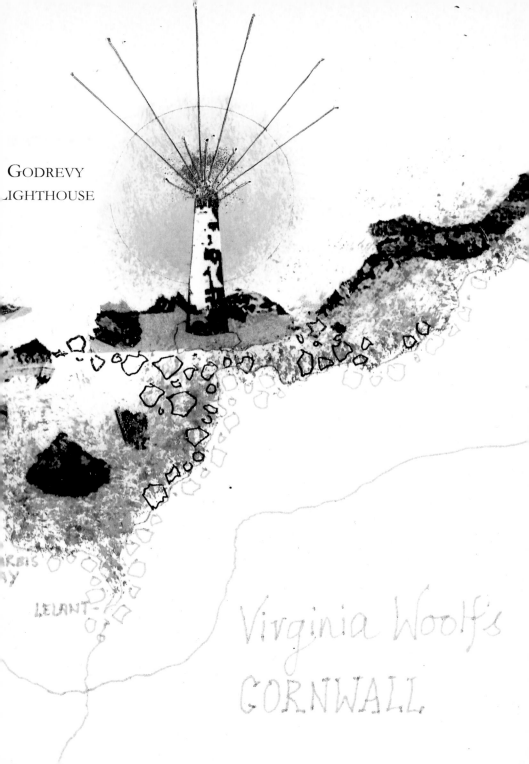

GODREVY
LIGHTHOUSE

ARBIS
AY

LELANT

Virginia Woolf's
CORNWALL

To the Lighthouse

Jacob's Room

The Waves

TALLAND HOUSE
Maggie Humm

Of all her houses, Talland House is the most significant in Virginia
Woolf's life and work. The house and St Ives landscape appear in her
major modernist works: *Jacob's Room*, *To the Lighthouse* and *The Waves*, where
'the sea was indistinguishable from the sky, except that the sea was slightly
creased as if a cloth had wrinkles in it' (TW 3). *A Sketch of the Past*, Woolf's
haunting memoir written near the end of her life, devotes pages to her
memories of spending thirteen glorious summers in Talland House
between 1882 and 1894. In *A Sketch*, St Ives is her first memory 'Of red
and purple flowers on a black ground – my mother's dress... and I was on
her lap... Perhaps we were going to St Ives; more probably, for from the
light it must have been evening, we were coming back to London' (MOB*
64). As soon as they arrived, the children would run wild down the steep
lane to Porthminster Beach where Virginia learned to swim. Her mother
Julia Stephen watched, as Virginia scrambled over rocks to find red and
yellow sea-anemones, and small fish flapping in pools across the wide bay.
A visiting friend, the writer J. A. Symonds, thought the bay akin to Naples.

Her father, Leslie Stephen had found Talland House on a walking tour the
year before Woolf's birth, and 'when they took Talland House father and
mother gave us – me at any rate – what has been perennial, invaluable'
(MOB 128). Leslie bought the land in front of the house to enable an
unrestricted view of the sea and Godrevy Lighthouse. The summer breaks
were long, from June to October, and the first mention of the house, in
May 1892, in the Stephen childrens' home-made newspaper *Hyde Park
Gate News*, reveals Virginia's adoration. 'The Stephens were going to St
Ives very much earlier than usual. This is a heavenly prospect to the minds
of the juveniles who adore St Ives'. In Woolf's memories the summers
were always hot, and she ate Cornish cream with blackberries.

*Moments of Being

The spaces of house and gardens are named and celebrated by Woolf in *A Sketch of the Past* and linked to key events and memories – a guest losing her brooch on the beach recurs in *To the Lighthouse* – the Talland House novel par excellence, although set in the Hebrides. A date of crucial significance was the 12th of September 1892 when Virginia sailed to Godrevy Lighthouse, leaving brother Adrian behind in Talland House, which becomes the opening scene of *To the Lighthouse*. Woolf's mother Julia Stephen 'was central... Talland House was full of her' (MOB 83). Woolf remembers her mother in a white dressing gown on the balcony, the sound of her bracelets as she taught the children their lessons on the dining room table. After Julia's death, marking the end of Woolf's childhood, Leslie gave up the lease of Talland House. The ghostly significance of Talland House is in Woolf's magnificent evocation of loss and presence in the 'Time Passes' section of *To the Lighthouse*. 'So with the house empty... What people had shed and left – a pair of shoes, a shooting cap, some faded skirts and coats in wardrobes – those alone kept the human shape and in the emptiness indicated how once they were filled and animated' (TTL 175-6). Woolf thought the novel portrayed 'the sound of the sea & the birds, dawn, & the garden' (D4 11 February 1931). The view of the lighthouse recurs again and again in Woolf's work. In *Night and Day* 'an odd image came to his mind of a lighthouse besieged by the flying bodies of lost birds' (N & D 378). Woolf's other recurring images – waves breaking on the shore, silver fish dangling, sails in the wind – all stem from her time in Talland House.

The St Ives light drew many artists to the town. St Ives' north-east to north-west aspect meant that the sun gleamed over the water in the morning and sank glowing into the sea in the evening. In retrospect, the Annual Regatta seemed to Woolf like a French painting. Woolf must have admired this light as a child because tropes of light flood her writing. Light functions in her writings, not as an abstract aesthetics but illuminates characters' everyday perceptions and creates a modernist sense of presence and absence.

Woolf continually marries the visual with gender. In *To the Lighthouse*, the artist Lily Briscoe subverts a masculine world-view – men's philosophical discussions about reality – with her visual imaginings. She genders and transmogrifies the men's example of a table into one 'scrubbed' by women, 'lodged now in the fork of a pear tree [with] silver-bossed bark [and] fish-shaped leaves' (TTL 23). The novel concludes with Lily's modernist portrait of Mrs Ramsay completed in a single brushstroke which enables Lily to have her vision.

The topology of *To the Lighthouse* mirrors Talland House and its gardens. Spaces there had names: 'the coffee garden', the 'rose garden', the cricket pitch. Stella Duckworth, Woolf's half-sister, in her 1893 diary describes painting with Julia in the rose garden. In Stella's photographs taken in that year, the windows and doors of Talland House are always open to the garden. Friends and family, including Symonds and Henry James, are photographed in that border space. There is a fluidity between house and garden landscape, full of movement with the eight children, servants, and guests. These records of Woolf's childhood have a haptic intimacy, replete with memory as well as a sorrowful aura.

Talland House and St Ives so infused Woolf's imagination that she returned again and again as an adult: in 1905 she peered through a window but 'the lights were not our lights,' Woolf had her fictionalised memories, and the delight in 1905 that 'at every turn of the road, we could anticipate some little characteristic... & great was our joy when we discovered our memory was right' (PA 282).

Maggie Humm is an Emeritus Professor whose work on Woolf includes *Feminist Criticism*, *Feminism and Film*; *Modernist Women and Visual Cultures: Virginia Woolf, Vanessa Bell, Photography and Cinema*; *Snapshots of Bloomsbury: The Private Lives of Virginia Woolf and Vanessa Bell*; and *The Edinburgh Companion to Virginia Woolf and the Arts*. Her novel *Talland House*, She Writes Press, takes Lily Briscoe from *To the Lighthouse*, telling her life outside Woolf's novel, and Lily solves the mystery of Mrs Ramsay's sudden death. *Radical Woman: Gwen John & Rodin*, a second novel, is forthcoming January 2023.

TALLAND HOUSE, ST IVES

I could fill pages remembering one thing after another.
All together made the summer at St Ives
the best beginning to a life conceivable.
When they took Talland House,
father and mother gave us
— me at any rate —
what has been perennial, invaluable.[1]

Virginia Woolf, *Moments of Being*

Artwork: Louisa Amelia Albani, 2022.
Photo: Vanessa, Julia, Virginia and Thoby Stephen
outside Talland House, St Ives, Cornwall, in the
summer of 1894. Smith College Libraries.

My mother would come out onto her balcony in a white dressing
gown. There were passion flowers growing on the wall;
they were great starry blossoms, with purple streaks,
and large green buds, part empty, part full.
If I were a painter I should paint these first impressions
in pale yellow, silver, and green. There was the pale yellow
blind; the green sea; and the silver of the passion flowers.
I should make a picture that was globular;
semi-transparent. I should make a picture of curved petals;
of shells; of things that were semi-transparent;
I should make curved shapes, showing the light through,
but not giving a clear outline.[2]

Virginia Woolf, *Moments of Being*

Artwork: Louisa Amelia Albani, 2022.
Photo: Julia Stephen (Virginia Woolf's mother) at her desk at
Talland House with a drawing by G. F. Watts of her mother,
Maria Pattle Jackson. 1892. Smith College Libraries.

The painter Lily Briscoe accompanies the botanist and old friend of the Ramsay family, William Bankes, on a walk in the garden:

So off they strolled down the garden in the usual direction, past the tennis lawn, past the pampas grass, to that break in the thick hedge, guarded by red-hot pokers like brasiers of clear burning coal, between the blue waters of the bay looking bluer than ever. They came there regularly every evening drawn by some need. It was as if the water floated off and set sailing thoughts which had grown stagnant on dry land, and gave to their bodies even some sort of physical relief. First, the pulse of colour flooded the bay with blue, and the heart expanded with it and the body swam, only the next instant to be checked and chilled by the prickly blackness on the ruffled waves. Then, up behind the great black rock, almost every evening spurted irregularly, so that one had to watch for it and it was a delight when it came, a fountain of white water; and then, while one waited for that, one watched, on the pale semicircular beach, wave after wave shedding again and again smoothly a film of mother-of-pearl.[3]

Artwork: Louisa Amelia Albani, 2022.

Nothing that we had as children made as much difference, was
quite so important to us, as our summer in Cornwall.
The country was intensified, after the months in London
to go away to Cornwall; to have our own house;
our own garden; to have the Bay; the sea; the moors;
Clodgy; Halestown Bog; Carbis Bay;
Lelant; Trevail; Zennor; the Gurnard's Head;
to hear the waves breaking that first night
behind the yellow blind; to dig in the sand;
to go sailing in a fishing boat;
to scrabble over the rocks and see the red and yellow anemones
flourishing their antennae; or stuck like blobs of jelly
to the rock.. to look over the grammar in the dining room
and see the lights changing on the bay.[4]

Virginia Woolf, *Moments of Being*

On Saturday morning
Master Hilary Hunt and Master Basil Smith
came up to Talland House and asked
Master Thoby and Miss Virginia Stephen
to accompany them to the light-house
as Freeman the boatman said that there was
a perfect tide and wind for going there.
Master Adrian Stephen was much disappointed
at not being able to go.[5]

Virginia Stephen
*Hyde Park Gate News**
12 September, 1892

Artwork: Louisa Amelia Albani, 2022.
Photo: Godrevy lighthouse from the beach at low water. Geograph.org.uk. Andy F.

* *Hyde Park Gate News* is a compilation of family 'newspapers' written by Virginia Stephen,
her sister Vanessa and brother Thoby.

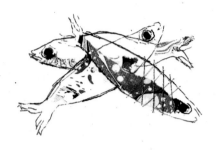

When we came near we saw that the enclosed school was of a deep and unmistakable purple; little spurts of water were flickering over the surface, and a silver flash leapt into the air for a second. We took up our places by the row of corks and waited; after a time the empty pilchard boats with their baskets drew up and let down a smaller net, called the tucking net, in the centre of the larger one, so that all the fish were gathered in a small compass. Now all the boats made a circle round the inner net, and the two boats who held the net gradually drew it up. The water within seethed with fish. It was packed with iridescent fish, gleaming silver and purple, leaping in the air; lashing their tails, sending up showers of scales.
Then the baskets were lowered and the silver was scooped up and flung into the boats; it was a sight unlike any one has seen elsewhere, hardly to be described or believed.[6]

Virginia Stephen diary entry, 1905

Artwork: Louisa Amelia Albani, 2022.
Photos: Penwith, Cornish coastline. July 2011. Lewis Clarke.
Portrait of Virginia Woolf. 1902. George Charles Beresford.

THE SEPTEMBER PILCHARD HARVEST

We have been walking among
the most remarkable moors,
among barrows, British villages,
stone maidens and beehive huts.
If it weren't for the excitability
of geese at night,
this would be the place
I should like to live in.[7]

Virginia Stephen letter to Clive Bell,
4 September, 1910

By looking over my left shoulder I see gorse yellow
against the Atlantic blue, running up, a little ruffled,
to the sky, today hazy blue.
And we've been lying on the Gurnard's Head,
on beds of samphire among grey rocks
with buttons of yellow lichen on them.
How can I pick out the scene?
You look down onto the semi-transparent water —
the waves all scrambled into white round the rocks —
gulls swaying on bits of seaweed —
rocks now dry now drenched with white waterfalls
pouring down crevices.
No one near us but a coast-guard sitting outside the house.
We took a rabbit path round the cliff,
and I find myself shakier than I used to be.
Still however maintaining without force to my conscience
that this is the loveliest place in the world.
It is so lonely.[8]

Virginia Woolf diary entry,
30 March, 1921

Artwork on previous pages and right: Louisa Amelia Albani, 2022.
Photo: Gurnard's Head promontory from the Coast Path to the east,
Cornwall (tinted sepia). Jim Champion. 15 August 2005.

GURNARD'S HEAD, CORNWALL

North of the hamlet of Treen in the parish of Zennor,
one mile to the west of Zennor Head

I observed the singular beauty of
leafless but budding trees
against a deep blue sea.
The sea is a miracle
— more congenial to me
than any human being.[9]

Virginia Stephen letter
to Clive Bell,
20 April, 1908

Artwork: Louisa Amelia Albani, 2022.

VIRGINIA IN RED & BLUE *with* BIRDS

Astra Bloom

Christmas Eve, 1909, Virginia catches the train from Paddington.
Why stay in London when Cornwall is going on?

To the sea and blue gold green. To the light of babies in Broderie Anglaise
under apple trees. A lighthouse, a father. Brothers, sisters. Wave upon wave.
Happiness. Mother in all. Mother is there, mother is gone. And he and he and
she. Paradise stopped. And they and there. And protecting her vision, like the
painter she'll birth, Virginia will be honest about bright violet.

Virginia, after breakdowns you'll walk on moors with ancients. You'll go low then fly over this
lovely dreadful world – shapeshifting to sudden prayer, a high bird, wet gold moss on Zennor
walls – and back – to You – dear Goat playing cricket – and foward – to You – in
Bloomsbury with friends and your words, and silk your favourite to wrap your precious body in.
Oh, on heavenly nights you hunted moths. There were stones with eyes, dazzle-dragonflies.
Virginia, you will make and unmake, rush in, flow out, again again.

The train speeds, a silver-black river and Virginia a fish.
Within the water she swims
deep where memories live. Till up she spurts, breaks the surface
into silver ruffles. Virginia is going back.
Without handkerchief, spectacles, cheque book or a coat,
but how marvellous that she goes, up and goes like that.
Virginia finds a spring night at The Lelant Arms.
Sits dreaming at her open window.
Morning reveals the beauty of the place,
views of the lighthouse, the grey mist bay.
Christmassing alone she climbs Trencrom in no coat,
perches upon a granite tombstone
in rain. Returns to a warm fire. Is alive.
Sitting room to herself on Boxing Day.
After the farmers and carol singers have gone to bed,
no moon or stars come out.
Virginia looks into the black fur night and shapes appear, and she
imagines herself
at the centre
of every thing. Each blazing soul, each dangerous rainbow day.

The living and the dead have flown down with her on the train.
And she has unfinished something, something silver flickers out
of reach and it cuts.

Sea, truth, love. Each protects, inspires, decimates. But.
Birds. Flocks. Soaring. Hovering.
Lonely sea-birds and fast, exact ones who swoop.
Their wings carry and sooth, carry and soothe,
as a mother with a lantern in a too-midnight room.
Go home.
Come back.
                    Voices.
She has gone back.

Love comes in waves and in white wings of light. Ghosts. Virginia does not walk
alone. See her plunge her bare feet in the Christmas Atlantic, red geraniums
blooming in her cheeks. In the salt-wind. They are here now, all still live.
Nothing has happened, everything is happening. Moments. Endings and
beginnings. Virginia has piled them all inside a sizeless cream cockleshell for
safe-keeping.

Searching transports her. A purple gold ache is a portal.
Bright fish in a fast stream in blue with a clever red hat but no coat.
What courage love takes, what hot coal, how strong an engine one needs.

Fast-slow rabbits, children running down to a blue bay. A yellow blind she hears
the sea behind. Red and purple flowers on her mother's dress. Being in the best
of places. First ecstatic memories.

Virginia, you wrote this all, the world, yesterday on a green seaside sofa whilst the tall birds
talked. Thank you. Merry Christmas.
Now close the doors and open the windows. And Listen. They are singing down there.

Astra Bloom writes fiction, poetry, plays and is currently working on an Arts Council
funded memoir project. Her work is published in journals, magazines and anthologies,
including *Common People: an Anthology of Working Class Writers* and *A Wild and Precious Life*
anthology. Astra lives in Brighton and is represented by Abi Fellows at The Good
Literary agency.

Extract from Virginia Woolf's novel
TO THE LIGHTHOUSE
inspired by Godrevy Lighthouse

Virginia's childhood boat trip to Godrevy Lighthouse, recorded in *Hyde Park Gate News* (a family 'newspaper' created with her young siblings) is echoed in the final section of her novel. Ten years after a planned trip to visit the lighthouse near their summer home, James, Cam and Mr Ramsay finally undertake the long-delayed voyage, sailing in a fishing boat with Macalister and his boy:

The sails flapped over their heads. The water chuckled and slapped the sides of the boat, which drowsed motionless in the sun. Now and then the sails rippled with a little breeze in them, but the ripple ran over them and ceased. The boat made no motion at all. Mr Ramsay sat in the middle of the boat. He would be impatient in a moment, James thought, and Cam thought, looking at their father, who sat in the middle of the boat between them (James steered; Cam sat alone in the bow) with his legs tightly curled. He hated hanging about. Sure enough, after fidgeting for a second or two, he said something sharp to Macalister's boy, who got out the oars and began to row.[10]

Artwork: Louisa Amelia Albani, 2022.

Bibliography

Andrews, K. *Wanderers: A History of Women Walking*. Reaktion Books, 2020.

Brown, J. *Spirits of Place*. Penguin, 2002.

Dell, M, Whybrow, M. *Virginia Woolf and Vanessa Bell: Remembering St Ives*. Tabb House, 2004.

Gillespie, Diane, F. 'Maps of her own: Virginia Woolf In and Beyond the Archives.' *Woolf Studies Annual*. Vol. 25, pp. 97–136. Pace University Press, 2019.

Hill-Miller, K. *From the Lighthouse to Monk's House: A Guide to Virginia Woolf's Literary Landscapes*. Duckworth, 2001.

Woolf, V. *A Passionate Apprentice: The Early Journals, 1897–1909*. Ed. Leaska, M. A. Mariner Books, 1992.

Woolf, V. *A Writer's Diary: Being Extracts from the Diary of Virginia Woolf*. Ed. Woolf, L. Persephone Books, London, 2017.

Woolf, V. *Jacob's Room*. Oxford World's Classics, 2008.

Woolf, V. *Moments of Being*. Ed. Schulkind, J. Pimlico, 2002.

Woolf, V. *The Diary of Virginia Woolf*. 5 Vols. Ed. Olivier Bell, A, with the assistance of McNellie, A. New York, Harcourt Brace, 1977–1984.

Woolf, V. *The Letters of Virginia Woolf*. 6 Vols. Ed. Nicolson, N, Trautmann, J. New York, Harcourt, 1975–80.

Woolf, V. *The Waves*. Introduction by Parsons, D. Wordsworth Classics, 2000.

Woolf, V. *To the Lighthouse*. Oxford World's Classics. Oxford University Press, 2008.

[Excerpts] reprinted with permission of The Random House Group Ltd

If you are interested in purchasing an artwork from this pamphlet, please contact: louisa.albani@gmail.com

References

1   Woolf, V, p. 128. 'Sketch of the Past' from *Moments of Being*.

2   Woolf, V, pp. 79/80. 'Sketch of the Past' from *Moments of Being*.

3   Woolf, V, pp. 18/19. *To the Lighthouse*.

4   Woolf, V, pp. 127/8. 'Sketch of the Past' from *Moments of Being*.

5   Woolf, V, 'Hyde Park Gate News', 1892. With permission from The Society of Authors as the Literary Representative of the Estate of Virginia Woolf.

6   Woolf, V, p. 293. *A Passionate Apprentice*.

7   Woolf, V, *The Letters of Virginia Woolf*.

8   Woolf, V, Vol. 2. *The Diary of Virginia Woolf*.

9   Woolf, V, *The Letters of Virginia Woolf*.

10   Woolf, V, p. 155. *To the Lighthouse*.